THE

DualProcess
Marketing©

Dr. P. Hughes

CONTENTS

PART ONE: The Origin of Dual Process Marketing   **5**

Two Systems, One Brain   5

The Biology of Marketing   9

PART TWO: System 1 and System 2   **15**

A Struggle Inside Your Head   15

Who Really Makes the Decisions   17

PART THREE: Dual Process Marketing   **22**

System 1 and System 2   22

Breaking the Cycle of Disillusionment   24

PART FOUR: System 1 and System 2 in Action   **33**

Marketing Stories   33

Availability and Evidence   37

Confirmation and Belief   40

The Price of Optimism   42

Knowing What You Don't Know   45

Real and Imaginary Patterns   48

When Simplicity is Too Simple   51

When Enough Really is Enough   54

The Dangers of Belonging   58

Your Ego Gets in the Way   60

Present and Future Marketing   63

Decision Fatigue   65

CONCLUSION: The Power of Dual Process Marketing   **69**

PART ONE:
The Origin of Dual Process Marketing

Two Systems, One Brain

Your business can't survive without marketing.

Yet for many businesses, even large corporations, it is marketing that *threatens* their survival.

The reason for this is simple: marketers forget that the means of delivering and receiving marketing messages, the human brain, is driven by emotion and laced with biases, which makes it prone to catastrophic errors in decision-making and judgement. These errors are especially dangerous when it comes to medium- and long-term strategic planning.

Dual Process Marketing (DPM) evolved to address these errors. It is:

●● The application of the psychology of decision making to the field of marketing communications; and

●● A marketing methodology based on an evidence-based analysis of how buying decisions are made.

DPM is based on the well-established premise in psychology that the brain is divided into two systems and that decision-making is affected by a number of cognitive biases and heuristics. While these systems have variously been known as feeling and thinking or emotion and reason, they became more widely known and accepted through the work of psychologists Daniel Kahneman and Amos Tversky.

Kahneman and Tversky opted for elegance and simplicity when they called these systems System 1 and System 2 and each of these systems has a clearly defined way of working:

System 1 is fast, automatic and largely unconscious.

System 2 is slow, analytical, methodical and conscious.

However, despite the fact that we can describe the operation of these systems, neither system functions in isolation. It is how these systems interact that determines the quality of the decisions we make. As Warren Buffet said:

"To invest successfully over a lifetime does not require a stratospheric IQ, unusual business insights or inside information. What's needed is a sound intellectual framework for making decisions and the ability to keep emotions from corroding that framework."

The same logic applies to planning marketing strategies, and when you are marketing a product or a service you cannot — EVER — make your strategic decisions as if you were buying that product: we buy on emotion and the only way to build effective marketing strategies is to use reason. This is not as easy as it sounds. Using System 1 is an ingrained habit and it's difficult to break because it allows us to make good or effective decisions with reasonably little effort. As Kahneman explains in *Thinking Fast and Slow*:

"...the division of labour between System 1 and System 2 is highly efficient: it minimises effort and optimises performance. The arrangement works well most of the time because System 1 is generally very good at what it does: its models of familiar situations are accurate, its short-term predictions are usually accurate as well and its initial reactions to challenges are swift and generally appropriate."

Malcolm Gladwell, in his best-selling book *Blink*, referenced studies of nurses, firefighters, intensive care doctors and many other professionals who make (mostly) good decisions under severe pressure when they don't have time to think. They rely entirely on System 1. Another example of fast, effective judgments from the same book is the work of John Gottman, whose studies on marital stability and divorce prediction over more than 40 years have shown that it's possible to predict the outcome of a marriage to 95% accuracy after watching a couple interact for as little as 15 minutes.

However, just because System 1 works *most of the time* doesn't mean it works well *all* of the time, and the reasons for failures in judgement and decision-making are that System 1:

●● Can't ever be switched off, and

●● Is driven by emotion, hardwired with biases and prone to make systematic errors.

It was the combination of many years of creating marketing strategies, and an awareness of these biases and their effects on marketing decisions, that gave rise to Dual Process Marketing. It is based on the premise that we are not only blind to the mistakes we make, but blind to our blindness.

This makes it extremely difficult for us to spot our errors without external intervention or a well-defined process to mitigate against them.

The operation of System 1 and System 2 is a function of the evolution of the human brain. Evolution explains why we rely on System 1, why we find System 2 so difficult and why we don't have the cognitive resources to continuously check the decisions we make for the errors that infect them. If DPM tells us *how* buying decisions are made and marketing strategies are planned, evolution explains *why* marketing exists.

The Biology of Marketing

The primary function of marketing is to maximise the probability that your products and services will be bought at volumes that enable your business to grow. In evolutionary theory this is known as replication, and every human trait, including System 1 and System 2, is the product of evolution. This means that traits are adaptations or ways we evolved to overcome threats to our survival and the most powerful tool our species has in this struggle for survival is the brain.

The process of attracting customers is structurally similar to the process of attracting mates in the natural world. In both cases, the process is driven by a need to display your genetic or commercial DNA to best effect, and that is why marketing exists. The means of doing this is using your brain.

The human brain is disproportionately large compared to the brains of the other great apes and it's expensive to run. It consumes about a third of our available oxygen and a fifth of our blood glucose. Given the importance of the brain to our survival, it makes sense that it evolved to function economically, and that is why System 1 makes most decisions. It's cheaper to think fast and to use experience, emotion and intuition to make decisions, especially when this way of behaving has been a major part of our overwhelming success as a species, which has seen us grow from a population of less than a thousand reproductive adults, as recently as 70,000 years ago, to dominate the planet.

However, a growing number of psychologists are subscribing to the view that our brains have evolved beyond what is necessary to ensure survival. They maintain that it's sex and the extravagant marketing displays that surround it that have led to the evolution of such over-sized brains. Smaller brains would suffice for survival, but big brains are better for showing off. The psychologist Geoffrey Miller wrote:

"Our brains are different from those of other apes, not because extravagantly large brains helped us to survive or raise our offspring, but because such brains are better advertisements for how good our genes are."

There is, however, a problem with the cost of advertising: it has to escalate over time if it is to remain effective. In nature, as in business, marketing doesn't stand still. Displaying yourself to best effect and the costs of doing it are trapped in an upward spiral of cost, and with rising costs comes the risk that there aren't sufficient funds available when they're needed. Those who can pay these costs survive. Those who can't raise the funds when they're needed face extinction. For genes and brands, the rules of the game are the same: fertility is in direct proportion to the ability to pay. In nature and in business, the ability to pay determines whether you can be trusted.

For example, in nature the reliability of a sexual signal is determined by its cost. Some of the most celebrated displays of genetic fitness among males are to be found among birds. The peacock's tail and the artistry of the bower bird evolved as sexual ornaments and females choose the best mate by working out the *authenticity* of the sexual signals they receive: the more a signal costs the signaller, the more difficult it is to fake, and the more truthful it will be as an indicator of genetic fitness. In other words, the reliability of a sexual signal is determined by its cost.

When building their bower, some male bowerbirds use sticks to create walls and roofs, while others collect bright objects and fruits from the forest floor and decorate the walls and gardens of their bowers. Thousands of objects gathered over an extended period of time go to make up the bower, and neighbouring males, each casting a watchful eye on their competitors, will take any opportunity to destroy the bower of a rival. When the females approach, the males try to entice them into their bower in order to mate. The females, however, are discriminating. They go from bower to bower assessing the genetic fitness of the males by inspecting their creations, sometimes tasting the colours that the male has used to paint the walls. It will usually take multiple visits to a number of bowers before the female chooses the genes she wants. They will typically be the genes that other females want, as many female bowerbirds — like peahens — choose the same males.

As costs rise, the risk to the individual life becomes greater. The elaborate plumage of the peacock makes him visible to predators and restricts his ability to fly in order to escape from them. In a competition where the rising costs necessary to demonstrate authenticity threaten to exclude some of the players, males have a vested interest in lying. If a male can convince a female that his genetic fitness is greater than it actually is, then he will increase his chances of reproductive success.

Fertility, then, is an exercise in marketing, and for every advert, press release and piece of content put out into the world promoting genetic fitness, the recipient will always come back with the same question, "*Can I trust the message?*"

Brands and the marketing tactics that build them act as ornaments or fitness indicators that tell the world who you are and what you stand for. They have values that they articulate through advertising, sponsorship, affiliations and the design of online and offline stores. A brand, according to Michael Eisner, the former CEO of Disney, *"is a living entity and it is enriched or undermined cumulatively over time, the product of a thousand small gestures"*.

If it is to survive, a brand has to adapt to fluid market conditions, technological developments, shifts in consumer preferences and changes in the commercial ecosystem of which it is a part. If it fails to do this, it pays the price that any living thing pays for adaptive failure: it becomes extinct.

The goal of marketing, and what matters, is that the DNA of your brand is passed from one generation to the next, and the arms race of brands is structured in the same way as any competition for mates. It is a zero-sum game where the winner takes all, and the challenge every business faces is that the marketing methods that brands use to attract customers will become more costly over time as they battle to increase their market share. Superbrands are simply a natural consequence of this evolution. When the French newspaper *La Presse* became the first to allow advertising on its pages in 1836, the ads were simple and cheap, but in 2008 Guinness spent over £10 million on a single television advert. More than 6,000 dominoes, 10,000 books, 4,000 tyres, 75 mirrors, 50 fridges, 45 wardrobes and 6 cars were destroyed in the making of a single commercial.

Power means power to propagate, and what matters is the quality of the spectacle we produce. The more costly the display, the harder it is for your competitors to fake it, and this capacity for escalation is what determines the success of brands in the theatre of propagation.

The goal of life is fertility and in every walk of life it is achieved in the same way. Costly signalling and the risks associated with it act as proof of authenticity. Authenticity gives status, and status opens the door to fertility. This, then, is *The Law of Marketing Fertility*:

COST → RISK → AUTHENTICITY → STATUS → FERTILITY

This Law governs the behaviour of businesses whose primary purpose is to propagate. The five elements of this Law are not static. Cost always escalates, which means that proving authenticity involves ever-increasing degrees of risk. Once the status that yields fertility has been gained, it has to be sustained. However, in a game of escalating costs, you have to keep moving just to stand still, and the pressure to sustain and enhance fertility is the primary goal of marketing.

When Apple was in decline, Steve Jobs said: "*There's no sex in our products anymore*," and he was right in ways that even he didn't fully grasp.

What was his solution?

Marketing.

However, most businesses do not have the resources to invest anything like the amount that Apple invested in repositioning its brand.

How, then, do you prove the authenticity of your message and differentiate yourself from your competitors?

The answer is simple: you *think* your way through the problem.

PART TWO:
System 1 and System 2

A Struggle Inside Your Head

System 1 buys. System 2 plans.

The key to successful marketing is understanding the role that System 1 plays in the buying process, and the necessity of deploying System 2 at the centre of the planning process. This, the first in a series of books on Dual Process Marketing, looks at how to approach strategic planning.

The reason System 1 makes most decisions is because your brain is expensive to run, and fast, automatic decisions consume less energy. However, this drive to conserve energy and think quickly is what gives rise to the many biases and heuristics that distort System 1's judgement. Your impatience to make decisions, to get on with it, to take chances and act on impulse, are all functions of System 1 and the emotions that drive it.

This is System 1 speaking:

●● *"I can't wait! I need leads now!"*

●● *"Let's do what we did last time. It worked once and it will work again."*

●● *"This campaign feels right. Let's go with it."*

Because System 1 is a product of evolution, it must work well most of the time, otherwise it wouldn't exist in the form it does. However, just because System 1 works well most of the time doesn't mean it works well all of the time. Every business needs the drive and energy of System 1. Effective marketing is about knowing which decisions to allocate to System 2. Typically, these are strategic decisions that involve medium- and long-term planning. Remember: System 1 buys; System 2 plans, and your challenge is to understand how System 2 can insulate you against basic marketing errors such as over-generalising from experience, being overwhelmed by information, and acting too quickly out of tiredness or too slowly out of fear.

The purpose of this book is to explain the roles System 1 and System 2 play in building effective marketing strategies that create a platform for sustainable growth. The only way to do this is to manage the relationship between them. That's why it's called Dual Process Marketing, and this book will show you how it works.

Who Really Makes the Decisions?

DPM is about understanding how System 1 and System 2 interact and how using System 2 to plan your marketing and evaluate its performance on an ongoing basis will increase the return on your marketing investment.

You already know that your brain is expensive to run, which is why the speed and economy of System 1 drive most of the decisions you make. You don't have time and your business doesn't have the resources to deliberate over every decision. That's what psychologists call Analysis Paralysis. However, failure to be aware of how biased your brain is and to know the difference between thinking like a buyer and thinking like a strategist means that you will not let System 2 take the time to develop your strategy. More importantly, you will not be aware how your biased thinking, on an individual and collective level is distorting, leading you into error. Most marketing plans either fail or under-deliver because the thinking behind them is, even if only in small ways, incomplete and the mechanisms for spotting it are absent.

Strategic marketing plans take time to produce. They require a slow, methodical approach based on evidence and insight. This conflicts with the constant commercial demand for immediate results. That's why most business owners, professional marketers and corporate board directors use System 1. The promise of quick results and fast returns is loud and insistent. You tell yourself what you want to hear. It's easy. It conserves energy. It's a habit and habits are very comforting. Using System 1 to make decisions feels natural and effortless — which, of course, it is!

When you come to make tactical or strategic marketing decisions, you'll do what every human being does and you'll tend to let System 1 take control and repeat past patterns of behaviour: if you feel you wasted some or all of the money you invested on marketing agencies, you'll hire a new agency or take your marketing in-house without being aware of the role that System 1 played in your previous decisions. Without that awareness, you are unlikely to improve your return on investment.

When System 1 is running your marketing, it becomes very difficult to learn from experience. Worse than that: it becomes almost impossible to learn that you're not learning!

If you hand over control of your marketing decisions to System 2, you'll be able to look critically and effectively at your previous decisions and understand why they didn't give you the commercial results you expected and what you can do to rectify the situation. The past doesn't have to be the guide to the future if you change your approach to the problem. Once you are aware of how unconscious biases can distort your marketing, you are far more likely to build your strategies on solid ground. Just because you've hired marketing agencies in the past and the results have been variable, it doesn't mean the same will happen in the future. What matters is that you let System 2 set your objectives. It's not enough to look at the wide range of internal and external factors that might influence your marketing, such as operational practices and the macroeconomic climate. What matters is that you look at yourself as you look at these factors, because there is a high probability that you will not be seeing them as clearly as you think. The ability to spot these unconscious errors is one of the main strengths of DPM. Failure to do so means — as research by The Chartered Management Institute discovered when it assessed 2900 managers — that turnover, productivity and growth will suffer.

When marketing underperforms, businesses, marketing professionals and agencies are all liable, so they justify disappointing returns on investment by descending into magical thinking. You'll know this has happened when you hear things like:

● ● *"We need more time."*

● ● *"The market's tougher than we thought."*

● ● *"Perhaps you were a bit over-optimistic in your forecasts."*

If you let System 1 run your marketing strategy, you will become even more cynical about marketing agencies. That will make you an even bigger loser in the future than you are now, because you need effective strategic thinking to succeed. But when cynicism overwhelms you, you stop strategic marketing activity and either waste money on ad hoc initiatives or flit from one agency to another.

As a business owner or marketing professional, you can't afford the luxury of a life spent letting System 1 drive your marketing. If your marketing is going to work, if it's going to deliver a return on investment by giving you a strong platform for growth, you'll let System 2 do the work.

System 2 delivers growth. It may take you down a number of wrong paths before you find your way again — but it will get you there in the end.

You can't choose how your brain works, but you can choose to learn how to make best use of it. Understanding Google algorithms, the principles of marketing integration, or how to automate your marketing are all easier than understanding how to build effective marketing strategies that can generate growth and achieve the objectives you set.

DPM is the best guarantee you can get that your marketing will deliver the results you want. Whether this is commercial growth or the internal dissemination of corporate environmental policy, DPM is the most effective way to do it. It is built on a marketing methodology that covers every aspect of marketing from decision-making psychology to the integration and automation of marketing tactics. Above all, your marketing strategy can only be optimally effective when it is built on an awareness of how System 1 and System 2 affect the planning process and its execution.

PART THREE:
Dual Process Marketing

System 1 and System 2

If you want to build marketing strategies that deliver tangible returns on investment, you have to integrate every tactic into a timeline with clear accountability and progressively more-refined degrees of evidence.

You can only do this when you understand:

- Most decisions are made by System 1.

- System 1 makes these decisions quickly, automatically and unconsciously on the basis of habit, emotion and experience.

- System 1 is not good at strategic marketing decisions. If you allow System 1 to take the lead you'll repeat patterns of behaviour resulting in disappointing outcomes until cynicism leads to commercial paralysis.

●● System 2 must be in charge of your marketing.

●● When System 2 is in control, you'll learn to pause and think before you act.

In other words, reflection and the use of evidence becomes a habit. When that happens you will have learned to manage the flaws in your own decision-making processes and your strategic thinking will become extremely effective.

Peter Drucker said:

"The business enterprise has two — and only two — basic functions: marketing and innovation. Marketing and innovation produce results; all the rest are costs."

He's right.

Nothing can be achieved commercially without effective marketing, and marketing can affect every aspect of your business. Whether you want a clear focus for your business, a strong platform for growth, a strategic shift within a department of a large corporation or a change of culture within a department or a business, marketing can deliver them all.

The power of Dual Process Marketing comes from its unique and proven ability to deliver any and all marketing objectives on the basis of integration, automation and methodical, strategic thinking — all of which is underpinned by a grounding in how effective decisions are made. You can possess voluminous knowledge about marketing in the Digital Age, but if you don't know how to manage System 1 or when to let System 2 take charge, you won't get the best out of the knowledge you have and your marketing will consistently fail to deliver your core objectives.

Breaking the Cycle of Disillusionment

The Gartner Hype Cycle is a graphical representation of the commercial journey taken by emerging technologies. Only those technologies that pass through all five phases of the Hype Cycle and reach the Plateau of Productivity, where mainstream adoption takes place, survive the journey.

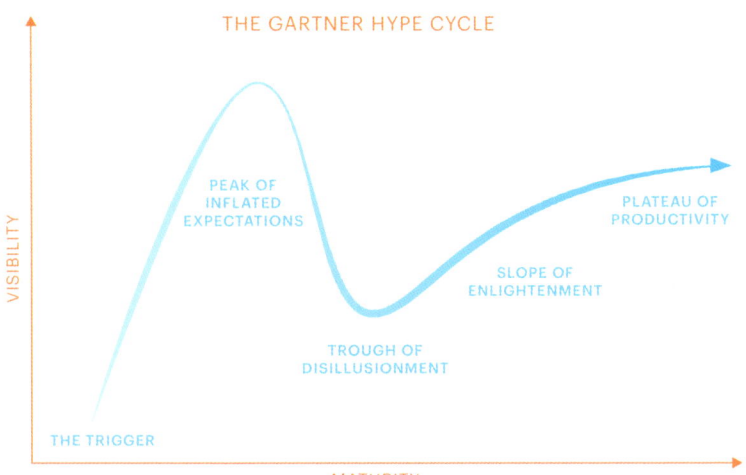

THE GARTNER HYPE CYCLE

VISIBILITY

PEAK OF
INFLATED
EXPECTATIONS

PLATEAU OF
PRODUCTIVITY

SLOPE OF
ENLIGHTENMENT

TROUGH OF
DISILLUSIONMENT

THE TRIGGER

MATURITY

Beyond its intended application to emerging technologies, the Gartner Hype Cycle is structurally a perfect representation of the commercial and psychological journey taken by businesses in relation to marketing. Let's look at each stage in turn:

The Trigger is driven by necessity. Marketing is an essential component of commercial success. If you want to grow your business to achieve any commercial objective, you have to invest in marketing.

Because System 1 drives most relationships between businesses, marketing professionals and marketing agencies, they all collectively rise to the Peak of Inflated Expectations. This happens soon after the beginning of the client/agency relationship. Despite the fact that all parties have all been there before, there is an inability to listen to System 2, or even to have an awareness of its existence.

Inevitably, everyone soon finds themselves in the Trough of Disillusionment. This is where the Player brings out his Box of Excuses (*"the market"*, *"the unexpected competition"*, *"Brexit"*, *"the global economy"*, *"man-flu"* etc...) and the Roar of Recriminations begins (*"I should have done it myself and never bothered with the agency"*, *"the client just won't listen to us"*, *"don't they know things always take longer than expected"* etc...).

It is in the Trough of Disillusionment that most client/agency relationships break down and confidence is lost in the ability of marketing to deliver tangible returns on investment.

However, because marketing has to be done, you begin the slow climb up the Slope of Enlightenment. At this point, you may be climbing alone or you may still have your marketing agency with you. In either case, everyone is bruised from the fall into the Trough of Disillusionment, and progress is slow.

If you make it up the Slope of Enlightenment, you arrive at the Plateau of Productivity. This is where your marketing begins to add value to your business. Sadly, not many businesses make it this far. They tend to sink into the Trough of Disillusionment and then go back to the beginning and repeat the same pattern. It would be funny if it weren't so tragic.

Of course, it doesn't have to be this way. DPM offers a very different structure to the journey that ends in delivering value out of marketing: it cuts off the Peak and the Trough. When you begin your marketing on a solid psychological footing, you know what you need to achieve your objectives, you're confident in the ability of your marketing strategy to deliver them and you recognise that a measured, methodical approach will get you where you want to go. Because System 2 is in charge, your expectations will be realistic and achievable. This, then, is what the DPM journey looks like:

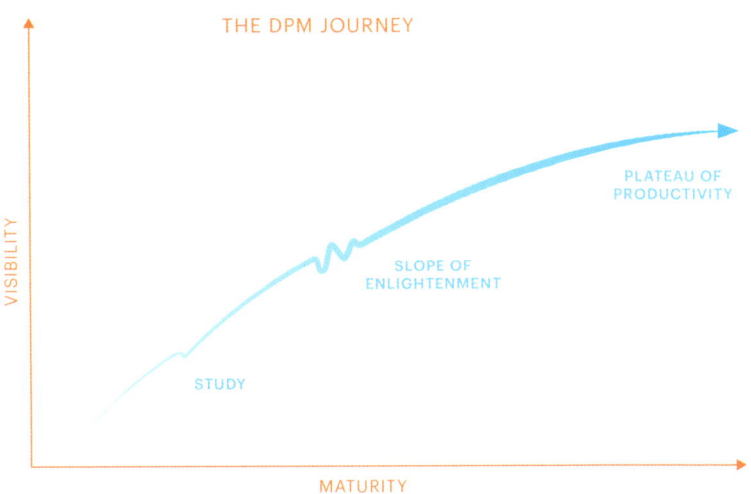

The reason that the lines are jagged in places is because effective marketing means knowing that some tactical decisions won't work and that you need a sufficiently robust strategy to correct them. This is made possible because the journey begins with a well-thought-out strategy. Breaking the Cycle of Disillusionment is not easy. It requires scepticism, persistence, lots of checklists, luck, and the ability to improvise. Let's look at them in turn.

Scepticism

Scepticism takes enormous cognitive effort, which is why asking difficult questions is a function of System 2. In one of the most famous studies ever made of how we believe what we believe, psychologist Daniel T. Gilbert proved that belief is far more natural to us than doubt. He showed that in order to understand an idea, we have to — often unconsciously — accept that idea as true. In other words, we believe before we doubt. Rejecting that idea is hard work and always happens after its automatic acceptance.

Belief is what System 1 does best. And that is what makes our plans so vulnerable to failure, which is why, if you want to create growth, you must use System 2 and base your decisions on evidence and, more importantly, on what you don't know. Awareness of ignorance is more vital to success than knowledge because that is what keeps your mind flexible and open to acting on evidence that contradicts what you believe.

Persistence

Success — personal, commercial, creative or financial — is always the result of persistence. The more mistakes System 1 makes and the more System 2 recognises and refines your behaviour, the more effective your fast, automatic thinking will become. If things don't go as planned, you'll learn to pause and reflect rather than react, and when you have to think quickly, your judgement will be more effective. Such behaviour is learned and when you need to change course or even abandon key elements of your marketing strategy, you'll act on the basis of accumulated evidence.

Your business can't grow without marketing — you have to keep going and there are many lessons in persistence from all walks of life. *Harry Potter* was rejected nine times before it was published, and if J.K. Rowling had quit after her eighth rejection, the landscape of modern publishing would be very different. Sometimes the consequences of rejection can be tragic. John Kennedy Toole was so distraught when his book, *A Confederacy of Dunces*, was rejected by publishers that he killed himself. Eleven years later, thanks to the determination of his mother, the book was published. It went on to sell over two million copies and won the Pulitzer Prize.

Checklists

Marketing strategists make problems of evidence and accountability more unmanageable than they need to be. That's because working without evidence is easier than working with it. Because System 1 is prone to making rash decisions which work well most of the time but not all the time, you need a mechanism for guarding against the complacency that comes from repetition and habit. That mechanism is the checklist.

The effective management of every aspect of your marketing strategy can be done via a series of simple checklists. Thanks to the work of Atul Gawande, the transformative power of checklists in areas as diverse as medicine and construction has become more widely accepted.

There is, however, an inherent problem with checklists from System 1's point of view: they're boring and they don't leave much space for heroism. Gawande writes in *The Checklist Manifesto*:

"(Checklists) provide a kind of cognitive net. They catch mental flaws inherent in all of us — flaws of attention, memory and thoroughness. It somehow feels beneath us to use a checklist, an embarrassment. It runs counter to deeply-held beliefs about how the truly great among us — those we aspire to be — handle situations of high stakes and complexity. The truly great are daring. They do not have protocols and checklists. Maybe our idea of heroism needs updating."

A great example of the primacy given to the heroism over discipline and routine is the case of Chesley B. Sullenberger III. He was the pilot who was credited with saving the lives of 155 passengers when the US Airways plane he was flying crash-landed in the Hudson River. He was hailed as a hero, given a hometown parade and a $3m book deal, and a film was made about the event, directed by Clint Eastwood. Despite the accolades, Sullenberger was humble and honest in his assessment of what happened: *"I want to correct the record right now. This was a crew effort."*

It was procedures, protocols and the use of checklists that saved lives that day. When the crisis came, everyone knew what to do. They coped with the unpredictable because they had prepared for it. Gawande observes that it is this tedious, disciplined work that System 1 hates:

"Discipline is hard — harder than trustworthiness and skill and perhaps even than selflessness. We are by nature flawed and inconstant creatures. We can't even keep from snacking between meals. We are not built for discipline. We are built for novelty and excitement, not for careful attention to detail. Discipline is something we have to work at."

Keeping your marketing strategy effective doesn't have to involve reams of unintelligible spreadsheets or an endless pursuit of perfect evidence before action can be taken. Instead, it involves gathering sufficient evidence to begin the journey and having the necessary checks and balances to deal with the inherent unpredictability of markets. That is a job for System 2, and one of the primary weapons in the struggle for growth is a checklist.

Luck

To be successful you also need to be lucky. And to be very successful, you need to be very lucky. This truism applies as much to businesses as it does to individuals. When you read the stories of successful entrepreneurs or the evolution of the world's biggest brands, you will find that much depends on chance encounters, random happenings and unpredictable events. Where, after all, would most offices be if Dr. Spencer Silver hadn't accidentally invented the Post-It note when he was trying to stop his bookmark from falling out of his hymn book? And what might the world be like if Steve Jobs and Steve Wozniak hadn't had the good fortune to meet through a mutual friend?

Luck is, by definition, random. But not entirely so. Having a questioning mind and a present spirit, you will have the energy to keep going when things fail and the insight to know what to do to rectify them. That's when you can turn random events into lucky breaks. You cannot predict the future of your business — not even a month from now — but you can make sure you are aware of your knowledge, accepting of your levels of ignorance and prepared for any eventuality — including those that cannot be seen. And this brings us to improvisation…

Improvisation

The jazz saxophonist and composer Steve Lacy said, *"in composition you have all the time you want to decide what to say in fifteen seconds, while in improvisation, you have fifteen seconds."*

Knowing the difference between composition and improvisation is also the key to effective marketing. You can't afford to wait to gather enough evidence to guarantee success, because there is no amount of evidence that can you give you the certainty you crave. What you can do is gather sufficient evidence to begin the journey, and have the flexibility to react effectively when the journey takes you to unexpected places. You might assume that composition is down to System 2 and improvisation is down to System 1.

That isn't the case.

It takes years of practice and dedication to be able improvise well, and it is the most important skill to have if you want your marketing to achieve any of the objectives you have set. And this takes us to the heart of DPM.

DPM is an art and a science that blends the power of well-composed marketing plans with the skill to improvise around them when you need to. DPM helps businesses distinguish between what you can control (your rigour and your attitude) and what you can't (everything else!). When you do this, the methodical approach of System 2 will become so ingrained that it becomes the fast reaction of System 1. When that happens, you have made success as likely as it can ever be, and that is the power of Dual Process Marketing.

PART FOUR:
System 1 and System 2 in Action

*At a conservative estimate, System 1 is riddled with over 200 biases.
They evolved because in our deep history they were useful and they can
still be useful now. Given that System 1 makes most decisions, they often
act as effective shortcuts in our thinking. Often, but not always, and Part
Four looks at some of the most important biases and their effect
on marketing strategy.*

Marketing Stories

Marketing begins with a story.

The mathematician and economist Nassim Taleb said: *"Facts come and go. Stories stick."*

Stalin made the same point rather more dramatically:

"A single death is a tragedy. A million deaths is a statistic."

We are biased to believe the stories we hear, which is why you must tell a compelling story about your business and the products and services you sell. This is what enables you to turn targets into prospects and prospects into customers.

The key marketing question is: how do you tell your story and evaluate its effectiveness?

Because System 1 makes most decisions, you want to make up the best story you can, without paying much — if any — attention to the facts.

When this happens you will end up:

- Over-embellishing your story in ways that carry a high risk of damaging your brand.

- Telling your story uncritically.

- Forgetting that a story is a living entity that needs constant updating.

Because people buy stories, it's vital that you tell the story of your business well. This means using System 2 to tell your story in such a way that it will work commercially. A commercially-effective story is easily absorbed. It has structure as well as content, and its effects are measurable.

Marketing is about achieving commercial objectives, and to do that, your story has to take your prospects and customers on a journey that is as believable as it is compelling. That's why the story of your business should follow the classic three-act structure.

The three-act structure is well-evidenced and used by master storytellers throughout the world, whether they are Hollywood screenwriters, best-selling thriller writers or great biographers.

The three acts are:

- Set-Up.

- Confrontation.

- Resolution.

As the title suggests, the Set-Up is the foundation on which the rest of the story is built. In a commercial context, it tells the story of why your business was formed. Ideally, this will involve finding consumers or businesses that were being poorly served or ignored by the market. You spotted this gap and offered them a way out of their misery.

The Confrontation is the story of the challenges you faced in bringing your products and services to market. It's a story of envious competitors and a heroic struggle for survival, but your determination and the quality of what you have to offer kept you going when the odds were against you.

The Resolution is the ultimate triumph of your vision and persistence. The story ends with you occupying a strong position in the market with a clearly-defined proposition that makes it easy for your target customers to find you, see the value you offer and buy from you.

When you use System 2 to tell your story, you will:

1. Always remember that stories have a target audience. This sounds obvious, but few businesses adequately segment their audiences or understand the psychological triggers that will get them to listen to your story in the first place.

2. Understand that the story of your business is the frame within which everything else sits. No-one will ever buy your products and services if they don't buy your story first. There's a reason why every ideology, religious or secular, has a foundational story: they are suited to the structure of our brains. When a marketing professor at Stanford asked her graduate students to give a 60-second pitch, only 10% used the time to tell a story, while the rest used facts and figures. When the students were asked to write everything they remembered about the pitches, only 5% cited a statistic. A massive 63% remembered a story.

3. Never end your story with *"...happily ever after"*. It must end with a number. The number you are looking for is the commercial value of the story you're telling and there are many ways to calculate this number, including weighting the story against key buying markers on a scale of target personas. This is where you have to be ruthless and be prepared to alter or completely discard a story that is close to your heart. Always remember: people buy on emotion, which is why you must use reason to structure your story and to set the metrics through which the effectiveness of your story will be assessed.

Availability and Evidence

You can easily accept that acting on the information that most easily comes to your mind is not a sound basis on which to make marketing decisions. That, however, is how most marketing decisions are made. The process happens below the level of consciousness and when you do it, you will not know what has happened. It will feel like you have made a reasonable decision. You won't be aware that many decisions are made by System 1 on the basis of the information most readily available to you, without subjecting that information to critical examination.

When decisions are made in this way, these are the kind of statements you might hear:

- *"I remember it as if happened yesterday, and there's no doubt that everyone feels the same way about it."*

- *"We have to run the same campaign again, seeing as it did so well last time."*

🟠🔵 *"You've spoken to at least four customers and they're all saying the same thing. How much more proof do you need?"*

🟠🔵 *"You spent 30 grand with one marketing agency, 45 grand with another and you wasted more than 100 grand on the last one, so it's definitely time to stop. There isn't a marketing agency anywhere that will give you what you want and it's better to invest your money in something more tangible."*

🟠🔵 *"The strongest memories are always your best guide when it comes to planning for the future."*

These statements are clear indications that you are basing your marketing decisions on emotion, not evidence. If left unchallenged, this approach will undermine your ability to create commercially-effective marketing strategies. Just because an idea or an experience is at the front of your mind doesn't mean it's an indication of the best way to build a marketing plan. Experiences are like footprints, and the more intense or memorable the experience is, the more likely you are to give more weight to that experience when you come to make marketing decisions. The result is that you give a singular experience or cluster of experiences more importance than statistical evidence, and that will lead to money being wasted on tactics that are unlikely to deliver a tangible return on investment.

Statistically, the odds are overwhelming that you are one of the people who let the availability of easily-recalled experiences determine your judgement on where to spend your marketing budget. If you've done this, the odds are even greater that some or all of your budget was wasted.

Thinking is harder than feeling, and if you're in any doubt about how easy it is to influence and distort your judgment, a famous experiment was conducted in which one group of people was asked if Gandhi was older or younger than 9 when he died, while another group was asked if he was younger or older than 144. The answer to both these questions is obvious.

But then each group was asked what Gandhi's actual age was when he died. The group who had the number 9 in their heads estimated 50. The group with the number 144 estimated 67.

So, before you do any marketing, check you're not mistaking cognitively-available information for evidence.

Confirmation and Belief

Whenever you evaluate which marketing agency to work with or which strategic decision is likely to increase the chances of achieving your marketing objectives, you don't start your evaluation with an empty head, even if it sometimes feels like you do.

Your mind is full of beliefs, which affect your senses and, if left unchallenged, will determine what you see and hear. When confronted with any major decision, it is normal to feel anxious about the consequences of that decision, especially since outcomes are under our influence but not our control. This feeling is so strong, it is often impossible to dislodge and the result is a selective approach to information. Of all the information available to you, you choose the information that confirms what you want to believe. This process is automatic, unconscious and difficult to spot. It goes so deep that it distorts your senses and your judgement. The old adage, *"I'll believe it when I see it"*, does not describe the behaviour of a mind run by the Player. Rather, the opposite is the case: *"I'll see it when I believe it."*

When we believe — even moderately — in something, we see evidence supporting that belief wherever we look. Famous studies conducted by Bertrand Forer showed that a majority of his subjects believed a personality sketch was an accurate description of who they were. What they didn't know was that everyone had been given the same personality sketch. Similar results have been found when people are told that a personality description is based on their date, time and place of birth, when, in fact, everyone has been given the same description.

If, therefore, you let System 1 drive your marketing strategy, you'll base your decisions on what you believe without testing those beliefs. The reason you have done this in the past, and will probably do so again, is that System 1's judgements are fast, automatic and *unconscious*.

Always remember, you are blind to your blindness and without you even knowing it, you will use information to confirm what you already believe. It's one of the biggest reasons for marketing plans failing. Last year the Centre for Economic and Business Research found that poor marketing cost UK companies £122bn in lost sales. That number would have been significantly lower if marketing plans had been designed and built by System 2.

The Price of Optimism

When System 1 is making your marketing decisions, you know they're going to work. You can feel it.

There is, however, no such thing as certainty in marketing. Effective marketing demands a degree of scepticism. Optimism, if it's allowed to break free from the reins of evidence, is likely to cause a lot of problems.

Here are two examples of where optimism leads:

- At the beginning of WW1, the head of the French army, General Edouard de Castelnau, said, *"Give me 70,000 men and I will conquer Europe."* The problem was that every other general was making the same optimistic claim with equal sincerity. They were all wrong.

- Optimism leads to planning errors because it makes us frame predictions on likely outcomes around best-case scenarios. A classic example of this was the cost of the new Scottish Parliament Building. The original estimate for the cost of building the Scottish Parliament was £40 million. The final cost was more than 10 times that amount at £431 million.

When emotion is driving your marketing decisions, you are likely to believe that your marketing strategies will deliver growth, regardless of whether the rigour with it has been formed. For a marketing professional, optimism can cost you and your clients an awful lot of money. Here are three typical basic errors made by the optimistic marketer:

- You run a campaign and leads fall out of the sky so you run it again. It flops and you're sacked for wasting the company's money. You are left bemused and sink into victim-mode as you find ingenious ways to blame anyone but yourself.

- You decide you want marketing to achieve 10% growth. You rustle up some kind of justification for how this will happen. It doesn't. So next year you decide you'll achieve 20% growth to make up for the disappointment. Will you never learn?

- You start your new job as a Marketing Director and you hire an agency and you wait for the leads to stack up at your door. At the beginning you're certain then hopeful then disappointed then resentful then angry then you make the same assumptions all over again and hire another agency.

The pressure to be optimistic, cheerful and positive is overwhelming. It is often misplaced and damaging. It creates a climate of emotional unreality. In the 1980s, sociologist Hochschild asked a group of Swedish flight attendants to be always cheerful, optimistic and positive. First they got stressed and then they got ill. Try it yourself and you'll feel the same.

The economists Malmendier and Tate found that overconfident CEOs, driven by an optimism bias, took excessive risks. A marketing professional driven by the same bias would be more likely to ignore a multitude of flaws in their planning, especially the effect of competitor activity.

Finally, there is the curse of the overconfident expert. An example from economics will suffice: 11,600 forecasts of stock market returns by leading CFOs of the world's biggest corporations were no better than chance.

System 1 will bias your marketing strategy and if you allow this to happen you must prepare to be disappointed. Your under-resourced, over-optimistic budget will not bring in the hundred new leads a month you expected. Misplaced optimism and lack of critical thought is also what has driven you to hire one agency after another and believe their lead and sale projections, which were never grounded in reality.

Knowing What You Don't Know

Prior to the Iraq War, the US Secretary of State, Donald Rumsfeld, reframed an idea first developed by psychologists in the 1950s and his speech became so widely reported it became the subject of a documentary. Here it is in full:

Reports that say that something hasn't happened are always interesting to me because as we know, there are known knowns; there are things we know we know. We also know there are known unknowns; that is to say there are some things we do not know. But there are also unknown unknowns — the ones we don't know we don't know. And it is those in the latter category who tend to be the difficult ones.

Most marketing is driven by automatic, biased thinking and is based on what you know that you know. That's why you don't get the results you expect. Knowing what you don't know, and acknowledging there are things that you don't know that you don't know, requires a high degree of cognitive effort, which is beyond the capabilities of System 1.

For example, scientists will never know the exact number of species that have become extinct, because most species die without leaving a trace of their existence. Another good example of the limits of knowledge comes from software developers, who work on the basis of limited predictability because of the unknown number of feedback loops within the system.

In marketing, an example of a *known unknown* is a competitor bringing a product to market that undermines your customer base. As for *unknown unknowns*, these are things so rare that they're not believed to be possible until they appear — but even in these rare instances, a flexible marketing strategy driven by the analytical, evidence-based approach of System 2 will be able to absorb any sudden changes without the fear of collapse.

Our limited knowledge does not, however, mean that marketing activity is deferred. There are leads to be generated and sales to be made. You cannot afford not to do marketing, and all marketing has to begin with knowledge of your market, competitors and the multiple channels through which you need to promote and sell your products and services. This knowledge can come from research, data and even experience.

What matters is that you never stop doubting and questioning this knowledge. The aim of any robust strategy is to create a platform for us to know what we don't know, and to allow what we don't know that we don't know, to become known. Effective marketing is built on a foundation of scepticism, and that means accepting there will always be a lot more that you don't know than you do know, and the job of marketing is to make best commercial use of our ignorance.

The path to growth is slow and methodical. System 1, on the other hand, offers you easy solutions and comfortable certainties. Optimism and certainty are a dangerous partnership and they make it impossible for you to see the inevitability of future losses and the past mistakes that led to them.

It's irrational to let System 1 be in charge of marketing strategy, but that's what most businesses do *because they are unaware it's happening*. They want fast results and they resort to fast, automatic, habit-driven behaviour. Even businesses whose services depend on an analytical approach that demands research, data and patience (for example, technology, engineering, construction, software etc.) often treat marketing as if it's a kind of magic. They set a budget, hire an agency, take cognitive short-cuts in the planning process and expect growth to happen.

If you want marketing to achieve your core objectives, you have to apply the same rigour to marketing as you do to other areas of your business. And that means allowing System 2 to do the work.

Real and Imaginary Patterns

The human brain evolved to identify patterns in the natural world and in human behaviour. This capacity has obvious evolutionary advantages, and in a commercial setting it's an indispensable skill in mapping customer behaviour, identifying changes in the market and refining your marketing strategy. The key question is: how do you differentiate a real from an imaginary pattern?

Here are some examples of non-existent patterns that people have believed in:

●● In 2006, Rhonda Byrne published a book called *The Secret*. It claimed to provide proof of the existence of a hidden *Law of the Universe*. She called it *The Law of Attraction*, which is a bit like karma: if you do good things, the *Universe* will reward you; if you do bad things the *Universe* will punish you. Byrne proved her thesis by telling lots of stories about people who thought positively and got what they wanted. Because System 1 makes buying decisions and is easily influenced by stories, the book became one of the best-selling books of all time.

A man who won the jackpot on the Spanish lottery claimed that he knew he was going to win because the last number he chose was 48. He chose that number because he'd dreamt seven times about the number seven and, as he told the media, *"seven sevens are 48"*.

Leonard Koppett predicted trends on the stock market correctly for 18 years out of 19. He claimed to have a revolutionary method that practically guaranteed investment success. He was believed and touted as an economic genius until he revealed that he was a sports journalist and his method was making decisions based on Super Bowl scores.

An expert in financial investments, a financial astrologer, and a five–year–old girl called Tia were asked to pick shares that they thought would perform well. The expert based his decisions on his knowledge of the markets. The astrologer based her decisions on the dates that companies were founded. Tia, on the other hand, was asked to catch papers with company names written on them, which were thrown from a balcony at Barclays Stockbrokers. When the predictions were analysed, Tia was the only one to make a profit.

When it comes to strategic thinking and planning, fast, automatic thinking will lead you into error. When you confuse a random event with a pattern, a story with a fact, you will not get the outcome you want. There is no doubt that you can think of plenty of examples of successful marketing tactics, but if you want to turn isolated successes into sustainable growth, you have to know the difference between a singular event or a series of events and a statistically-significant pattern. If you can't do that, you'll expect amazing results on the back of a few plausible stories.

Marketing is about probabilities and you can never be certain what's going to happen in the future because you have less control over outcomes than you think. However, you can influence outcomes, and that's what good marketing does. It uses evidence and feedback loops to see real patterns, and on the basis of these patterns, you can make it much more likely that you'll get a good return on your marketing investment. Probability can be leveraged.

Identifying a commercially meaningful pattern means finding a middle way between continuously gathering evidence so you can be certain you are right (which is impossible, because marketing doesn't deal with certainties) and driving forwards with insufficient evidence. When you have identified a pattern, you must test and refine it using System 2. The result will be a more-considered and less-biased marketing strategy, often with lower expectations. It may seem counter-productive to lower expectations when you want to grow your business. Surely you want to raise them, set yourself a high target and go for it! But the point is not to lower your growth target but your expectations. That way, you're more likely to build a strategy capable of achieving your target and spot the signs when it's not working. Expectations may create great enthusiasm but lead to even greater disappointment. Well-structured strategies get results.

When Simplicity is Too Simple

If you're a buyer, you want the marketing message to be as simple as it can be because System 1 is making the decision.

If you're a marketing strategist, too much simplicity will sabotage your efforts. And it's more difficult to fight the impulse towards a greater degree of simplicity because System 1 always speaks louder than System 2. There's also ample evidence to back up the drive to simplify the choices a customer has to make:

An experiment involved presenting two displays of different flavoured jams. One display had six different flavours, while the other display had 24. Shoppers spent about the same amount of time looking at each display, but when it came to making a decision to buy some jam, 30% of shoppers bought from the table with six flavours, while only 3% bought from the table with 24 flavours.

When you are confronted with too much choice, it's easy to feel overwhelmed, which can paralyse the decision-making process, and this experiment shows that too much choice hampers decision-making.

But you are not a buyer. You are a marketing professional or business owner who wants marketing to deliver growth or an agreed set of tangible objectives, and when complex, strategic marketing problems are resolved by System 1, the solution is likely to be over-simplified. That's why we opt for easy marketing solutions when there aren't any.

Substituting a complex problem for a series of superficial generalisations based on past experience and received knowledge is typical of the way many marketing decisions are made. Simple problems are always easier to deal with than complex ones, especially when the complex ones involve a lot of cognitive effort.

For example, an experiment was conducted to see what type of insurance people were most likely to take out while they were travelling abroad: insurance to cover death by terrorism or insurance to cover death by any means. Most people chose insurance to cover death by terrorism only, even though death by terrorism was obviously covered in *death by any means*. The reason people failed to see this was because their judgement was clouded by fear. They let fear simplify the calculation they made, and if they hadn't done that, they would have been able to make the decision rationally and come to a better solution.

Another example of the drive to find simple solutions to complex problems was the way the Brexit referendum debate was conducted. Complex economic, social, political and psychological issues, which cut to the core of the idea of individual and national identity, were reduced to a simple choice of what we fear most:

- Being cut off from the rest of the world and left to sink in a sea of isolation; and

- Being overrun by vast hordes of immigrants from all corners of the world.

The problem for strategic marketing then is an obvious one: while simplicity and clarity are clearly desirable in any strategic plan, they mustn't blind us to how difficult and challenging it is to create a marketing platform capable of delivering growth. It is the collusion between agencies and their clients in mismanaging this complexity that has tarnished marketing as a profession. Strategic marketing is about gathering qualitative and quantitative evidence; identifying multiple personas; integrating diverse marketing disciplines; being precise and diverse in the use of language; understanding the psychology of individuals and markets; knowing how to create a functional whole out of sales and marketing; and being able to differentiate between randomly generated information and meaningful data. Above all, marketing is about knowing that any conclusions are never more than provisional and will, at least in part, be erroneous.

When Enough Really is Enough

"If at first you don't succeed, try, try again. Then quit. There's no use being a damn fool about it."

That was the advice of actor and comedian W. C. Fields.

It's good advice.

Then why don't we take it? Why do we compound commercial losses beyond the point when we said we would stop? Why do we stay in marriages that we should have left years ago? Why, when we go the cinema, do we sit through an entire film, even when we know after the first 10 minutes that we're not going to like it? Why do we persist with marketing that is not delivering the results we want?

We do all these things because avoiding losses is more important to us than making gains. We hate losing more than we enjoy winning. You know that this is irrational, because an amount of money is worth the same whether you're avoiding losses or making gains, and your emotional approach will stop you from evaluating a situation with a clear head.

Many experiments have shown, however, that losses generate stronger emotions and influence our decisions more than gains. In one experiment, participants were told they had spent $100 on a good holiday, and $50 on a great holiday that they had found after they'd booked the first one. When they were told the two holidays overlapped, most participants chose to cancel the great holiday even though they would have enjoyed it much more. Why? Because they gave more emotional weight to losing $100, regardless of the better experience they would have had on the great holiday.

In another experiment, subjects were told they were going to see a film that cost $10, but when they got to the cinema they realised they had lost $10 from their wallets. Only 12% said they would not go in and see the film because of the loss of $10. But when they were told they had lost the ticket, 54% said they would refuse to buy another one. The loss in each case was identical, but it felt greater in the second. This is System 1 driving decision-making, and when this happens, decisions are not made rationally. The more time, money or emotion you invest in something, the harder it is to quit, because the losses seem disproportionately large.

One of the most famous examples of the inability to accept losses after a large investment has been put into a project comes from 1950s America and a Chicago housewife who went under the name of Marian Keech. Marian claimed to be receiving messages from extra-terrestrials known as The Guardians. These messages were given to her through automatic writing, and she soon had a small and devoted following called *The Brotherhood of the Seven Rays*, who believed a flying saucer would come to earth and save them when the world ended by flood on 21st December 1954. The night of the 21st passed without incident and the believers woke up to find the world intact, when they had lived their lives in the belief that it would end.

Given the clear proof that their beliefs were wrong, how many members of The Brotherhood lost their faith in Marian Keech and her prophecies? If you understand how the brain works and how emotion and gut feeling drive your decision making, you will know the answer. If you're in doubt, this is what the psychologist Robert Levine said happened to The Brotherhood when the prophesied flood didn't occur:

"Keech became elated. She said she'd just received a telepathic message from The Guardians saying that her group of believers had spread so much light with their unflagging faith that God had spared the world."

As a result, only two of the group left. The others became more fervent in their belief. Why?

There are many reasons. Here are a few of them:

- They had invested so much time and energy in The Brotherhood that the emotional and psychological cost of leaving was too big for them to accept. System 1 would not countenance such great losses.

- When we invest heavily in something and reality disproves the fantastic story that underpins our beliefs, we will not change those beliefs. On the contrary, we will change the nature of reality.

- When you commit to something or someone, it's hard to quit. So when the basis of this commitment is challenged, you react by strengthening your commitment, regardless of the evidence you are faced with.

If you want your marketing to work, you have to know when to quit a loss-making strategy and find a better solution. Failure to do so will simply compound your losses, and building flexibility into a strategy is not enough. You have to be prepared to act when the evidence tells you to change course. What makes this particularly difficult is that the tactical decisions being discarded will not (usually) be completely flawed. The evidence will be subtle but conclusive, and those are precisely the conditions in which the necessity to change meets the highest resistance. Typically you will say, *"Give it a little more time and I'm sure things will improve."* There will be times when people do give it more time and things do improve, but that's just one story and does not constitute evidence on which to build your strategy. Always remember: marketing judgements are based on probabilities, and that's why you should always ignore the exceptional story. I'm not saying you should quit just because the going gets tough — perseverance is essential to marketing success. What I'm saying is, you should quit when the odds are that you will incur even bigger losses than the ones you have already incurred.

The Dangers of Belonging

Human beings are social animals. We evolved to live and die in groups. This explains why researchers at Harvard University found that loneliness is as dangerous to our health as smoking. There are few things that people fear more than being isolated from the group, which is why you need to feel supported in your decisions and why you find it difficult to make unpopular decisions or to stand alone in an argument. You worry about being wrong or made to look like a fool, or losing your job and your friends. You imagine catastrophic consequences and these can overwhelm you and drive you to react without taking pause to think of a more constructive response.

One of the first and best experiments that show how our need to belong distorts our decision-making was done in 1951. Eight people were shown a line and asked which one of three other lines was the same size. The answer in each case was obvious, but of the eight participants, seven were stooges in league with the experimenter and had agreed their answers in advance. On 12 out of 18 occasions, the stooges gave the wrong answer.

That left the real participant with a choice: to say that the other seven were wrong and risk ostracisation from the group, or to give a wrong answer and conform to the group. 75% of participants conformed at least once.

Conformity can also take a darker turn. 24 Stanford students were asked to participate in an experiment. A mock prison was built and 12 of the students were told that they were guards and the other 12 were to be prisoners. The experiment was abandoned after six days because the guards had internalised their roles and were becoming increasingly abusive to the prisoners.

We have to belong to something, but you mustn't let belonging distort your thinking. It's common for marketing teams to want to believe in the value and integrity of the products and services they promote. It's also likely, because System 1 is driving their decisions, that they'll want to find agreement as quickly as possible, and that's when their desire to sustain the cohesiveness of the group and their shared assumptions will distort their judgement. So when they are presented with evidence, they will collude in an interpretation of the evidence that causes the least disturbance to the strategy they have all agreed upon.

You cannot afford to run your marketing in this way.

Your Ego Gets in the Way

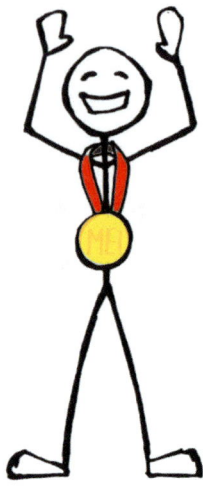

Nothing gets in the way of effective marketing more than your ego. The feeling that you deserve better results from your marketing, after all the time and money you've invested in it, can be very powerful. That's why when mistakes happen you'll find anyone to blame except yourself. You might even have a gold statue of yourself on your office desk and take time out of every day to polish it.

Vanity is one of the main reasons why you are unable to evaluate the decisions you make with a cool, clear head, and the evidence suggests that we all overestimate our own abilities, often to an alarming degree. In one study, over 90% of motorists believed they were better-than-average drivers, but there's a darker side to our vanity. When we judge other people's behaviour, we tend to put their behaviour down to their personality, even when circumstances are completely out of their control. This was shown when participants in an experiment were asked to read essays for and against Fidel Castro, and then to assess whether the writers were genuinely for or against the Cuban revolutionary leader. They were then asked the same question when the position that the writers took on Castro was decided by the toss of a coin. In both cases, the majority of participants believed the pro-Castro writers were personally approving of him. In other words, little consideration was given to the fact that the views of the second group of writers were entirely random.

What this shows is that when we evaluate other people's decisions and beliefs, we attribute the causes to their personality, but when we look at ourselves we always have an excuse for our behaviour that has nothing to do with our personal qualities. When we look for a reason for our own mistakes, we focus on circumstances not personality. When we make a mistake at work, it's because we're under pressure or the boss is having a bad day or our workload is unreasonable. In other words, it's the situation that makes us behave in the way we do. But the same doesn't apply to others. If other people make a mistake at work, we say: *"I can't believe he could be so stupid!"* or *"Won't she ever learn to do things properly,"* or *"What an idiot!"*.

If you still have any doubts about whether this applies to you or not, remember the last time you got annoyed when another driver cut you up. You didn't think it might have been an honest mistake. You reacted angrily, judging the action as a flaw in the character of the other driver. But when you cut someone up, it's always an understandable misjudgement and you get annoyed that the driver who you cut up is getting annoyed with you.

That doesn't mean you shouldn't stand up for yourself or make as strong a case as you can in defence of your own judgement. But the best way to value yourself is not to validate your fast, emotional reactions, but to value your ability to pause, think, reflect and reach a mature understanding of what's happening.

However, this conflicts with the primary goal of marketing, which is to tell the world how great you are. A world-beater. The best in the industry.

And isn't there a risk that while you pause, your competitors will steal your customers from under your nose?

Of course, you need to present your products and services as powerfully as you can in as many channels as there are available for you to do so. But you also need to pause. This doesn't mean you do nothing. What it means is that you suspend naive belief in your own wisdom and recognise that vanity, however unconscious it may be, will undermine your capacity for strategic marketing planning.

The key point to remember is that you want your buyers to idealise your business, but that you can't afford that luxury. You have to look at your business as it really is, and if you have the courage to do this, you'll soon find that the gap between the ideal and the real is much smaller than you think.

Present and Future Marketing

When you let System 1 dictate your strategy, marketing will be about the present. It's what you do now that matters, not what you might do next year or the year after. Things change far too much for us to predict the future, and you need leads now, so that's where all your resources should go.

System 2 would agree that marketing has to concern itself with the present. Businesses need constant growth and if they stand still, they go backwards. But it's a strategic error to discount the future just because it can't be predicted with certainty. In fact, the only thing you can know with certainty is the past.

Last week you may have had 10 enquiries, but that doesn't mean it will happen this week, even if it's happened every week of this financial year. It may be very likely that it will happen, but probability isn't certainty. And there lies the problem. You can't even predict the immediate future with certainty, and because of that you're always looking for a quick win. You may get it this week and next week, but at what cost? Unless you have developed a marketing strategy capable of sustaining you in the long term, eventually you'll run out of luck and the quick wins you expect in the future, but haven't planned for, won't happen.

It's careful strategic planning, driven by System 2, that generates greater commercial growth. According to Mintel, the ROI of future-focused, strategic marketing activity is 42% higher than tactical activity focused on short-term needs. If you listen to System 1, you'll believe you face a binary choice: either you focus on what you need now or you focus on the future. When you put System 2 in charge, you'll know that marketing delivers better short-term results if the activity is based on a long-term strategy. Why, then, do we listen to System 1 more often than we listen to System 2?

The answer lies in the many experiments that prove our preference for immediate — as opposed to deferred — gratification. Perhaps the most famous demonstration of this was conducted by Walter Mischel and Ebbe Ebbeson. More than 600 children were given the choice between having one marshmallow immediately or a second marshmallow 15 minutes later. The reactions of the children when the experimenters left the room showed how difficult they found it to defer gratification. Some covered their eyes while others touched and even stroked the marshmallows. A few couldn't defer at all and ate the marshmallows as soon as they were left alone. When the experimenters returned, only a third of the children had not eaten their marshmallow.

When the subjects of this, and similar studies, were followed up years later, the children who had successfully deferred gratification were found to be more competent and achieved higher SAT scores. In later life, they went on be more stable in both their personal and professional lives.

In marketing, if you want leads now, the best way to get them is to have a strategic mindset, and that means keeping the future at the front of your mind.

Decision Fatigue

One of the main reasons that System 1 makes most decisions is because the brain is expensive to run. Usually those decisions are good enough, and you want a life of cognitive ease. While most people can accept that they don't reason well when they're exhausted, you may be surprised to learn that even mild hunger or thinking hard about two different subjects in succession can lead to poor decisions.

When the decision making of eight parole judges was examined, the results were frightening. The perceived justice of the legal system in any free society is assessed by the consistency and fairness with which judgements are made. We expect judges to assess evidence in a rational, even-handed way across multiple cases. However, when applications for parole were put before these eight judges, a disturbing pattern emerged. In total, 35% of parole requests were approved, with 65% of those approvals occurring just after the judges had eaten. The number of approvals gradually reduced the further they were from the judges' last feeding, until they were almost zero immediately before the next meal. The hungrier the judges were, the less likely they were to grant parole. There are two reasons why this happens:

- Thinking consumes energy and when we feel depleted we are more likely to maintain the status quo rather than think through the consequences of change.

- Any effort of will is tiring.

In another example of the same phenomenon, participants were asked to stifle their reactions while watching an emotionally-charged film. Then they were asked to maintain a strong grip on a dynamometer for as long as they could. Those who had used an enormous effort of will to stifle their emotions found their physical stamina was reduced and they were unable to hold a firm grip for long.

A final example: People were asked to remember seven digits and while they were in the process of trying to do this, they were asked whether they wanted a chocolate cake or a fruit salad as a dessert. The majority chose the chocolate cake because you will always look for comfort when System 2 is making you think slowly and hard. Any activity that consumes cognitive energy will result in a need for respite, which usually means making a quick decision. We have limited energy, and faster decisions conserve more energy. That's why we like our decision-making process to be fast and efficient rather than slow and expensive.

This dichotomy is, however, an illusion. The faster you think, the less energy you use — but that doesn't mean you make better decisions. On the contrary, fast thinking leads to overspending; poor financial management; short-term expediency; unnecessary aggression; impulsive behaviour; and poor, inconsistent decisions.

Let's assume you have an ambitious growth target of 25% year-on-year. Before any marketing begins, you have three major problems to face:

- Three years is too far in the future to be psychologically meaningful.

- The present demands for leads and sales will occupy a far stronger position in your mind.

- The greater marketing investment has to be focused on achieving the long-term growth target, because that's where the greater commercial value lies.

- However, System 1 has the strongest influence on your decisions and will pull you towards the cognitively easiest option, which is to focus on the present.

This is the exhausting cycle of conflicting demands on your attention that every business has to face on a daily basis. System 1's ultimate triumph in this competition for cognitive resources is one of the main reasons why clients and marketing agencies fall out. An effective agency will be able to put a strategy in place that will deliver progressively greater commercial returns as time passes, without damaging the top line in the short term. However, because by definition long-term strategies are geared towards future success, there comes a moment in time when the demand for instant results becomes more insistent. This is the marketing equivalent of a fever. It's a crisis point from which the marketing strategy will either be strengthened because of the ordeal, or it will die.

Conflicts between client and agency are tiring, and if either or both parties opt for short-term fixes, it won't be long before client and agency agree to part company, often acrimoniously. And yet another nail is banged into the coffin of effective marketing.

CONCLUSION:
The Power of Dual Process Marketing

System 1 and System 2 cannot exist in isolation from each other.

They evolved together because they both serve useful functions, and if marketing is to achieve its principal objective — which is the replication of products and services — you have to learn how to manage the biases that distort System 1 thinking, while still being able to make fast decisions when you need to. The goal, therefore, is to incorporate the slow, methodical thinking of System 2 into the gut feeling and automatic reactions of System 1. In other words, you have to develop an instinct for evidence-based thinking, and that can only happen after repeated practice.

The best analogy is chess. International master and cognitive psychologist Dr. Fernand Gobet studied hundreds of chess players and concluded that the average chess expert spent an average of 1.03 years of serious practice, while the average master spent an average of seven years. Stronger players were also more likely to have a coach and to read more chess books than weaker players. They also started playing chess seriously at 10–12 years of age, while experts started later at about 14.

All this slow, deliberate practice enables masters to identify patterns faster and more accurately than weaker players. They will learn several hundred thousand perceptual chess patterns, which explains their fast, automatic discovery of good moves as well as their exceptional memory.

The fact that chess is played with a board and 32 pieces, with a finite time-budget, makes it a wonderful vehicle to study decision-making. In chess there are good decision-makers and bad decision-makers, and the difference between the two can be seen in their ELO ranking (i.e. a method of calculating the relative strength of chess players). Former World Chess Champion Gary Kasparov affirmed the power of chess as a laboratory for analysing decision-making:

"...it is due to its limited scope that chess provides such a versatile model for decision-making. There are strict standards of success and failure in chess. If your decisions are faulty, your position deteriorates and the pendulum swings towards a loss; if they are good, it swings towards a victory. Every single move reflects a decision and, with enough time, it can be analysed to scientific perfection, whether or not each decision was the most effective."

Commenting on Magnus Carlsen, the current World Chess Champion, English grandmaster Jonathan Speelman said:

"...he drives his opponents into errors. He plays on forever, calmly, methodically and, perhaps most important of all, without fear. This makes him a monster and makes many opponents wilt."

What applies to chess also applies to marketing: distinguishing between real and imaginary patterns; controlling emotion; managing the many biases that distort your thinking; and integrating the fast, automatic reactions of System 1 with the slow, methodical thinking of System 2 takes years of deliberate practice.

Dual Process Marketing is proof that it takes time to learn how to do effective marketing, and there is no end to that learning. Marketing, like every living thing, evolves. And Dual Process Marketing is the best guarantee you can get that you will stay ahead of the competition.

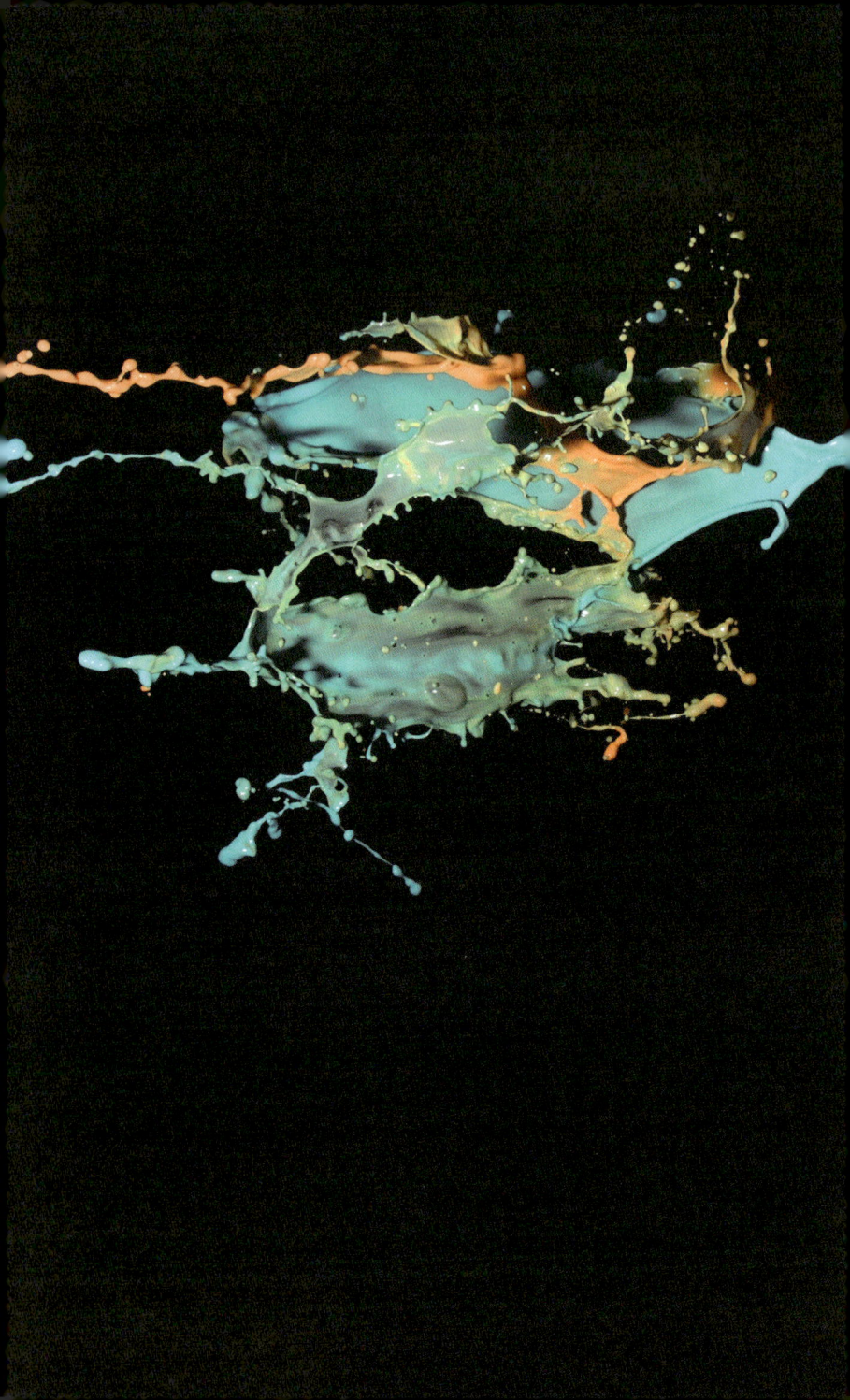

Printed in Great Britain
by Amazon